Vision and Values: organisational culture and values as a source of competitive advantage

John Purcell
Sue Hutchinson
Nick Kinnie
Juani Swart
Bruce Rayton

The Chartered Institute of Personnel and Development is the leading publisher of books and reports for personnel and training professionals, students, and all those concerned with the effective management and development of people at work. For full details of all our titles, please contact the Publishing Department:

Tel: 020 8263 3387
Fax: 020 8263 3850

E-mail: publish@cipd.co.uk

To view and purchase all CIPD titles:
www.cipd.co.uk/bookstore

For details of CIPD research projects:
www.cipd.co.uk/research

Vision and Values: organisational culture and values as a source of competitive advantage

John Purcell
Sue Hutchinson
Nick Kinnie
Juani Swart
Bruce Rayton

Work and Employment Research Centre, School of Management,
University of Bath

© Chartered Institute of Personnel and Development 2004

First published 2004

Cover design by Curve
Designed by Beacon GDT
Typeset by Paperweight
Printed in Great Britain by Short Run Press

British Library Cataloguing in Publication Data
A catalogue record for this book is available from the British Library

ISBN 1 84398 110 6

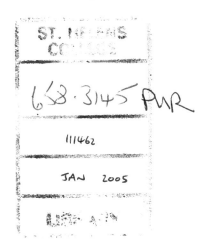

Chartered Institute of Personnel and Development,
CIPD House, Camp Road, London SW19 4UX

Tel: 020 8971 9000
Fax: 020 8263 3333
Website: www.cipd.co.uk

Incorporated by Royal Charter. Registered charity no. 1079797.

Contents

Foreword

This Executive Briefing draws on the data generated and reported in the CIPD research report, *Understanding the People and Performance Link – unlocking the black box*, to further discuss the importance of a strong vision and values to the relationship between HR practice and organisational performance. This was one of the issues that the people and performance research, carried out for the CIPD by Professor John Purcell and his team at Bath University, identified as being significant. Other issues such as the role of front-line managers in bringing policies and practices to life and the management of professional knowledge workers' careers have already been reported on in previous papers in the CIPD's Executive Briefing series.

The research team discovered that successful organisations are characterised by strong values and a strong guiding vision that communicates what behaviour is appropriate and what is not. The team also found that it is important that organisations create the kind of environment or culture where the positive managerial behaviours of listening, coaching, guiding, involving and problem-solving are actively encouraged and reinforced.

In many of the organisations the vision can be summarised as a 'Big Idea', which guides and shapes organisational activity. However, to be successful it not only needs to be embedded across the organisation and hence widely understood by everyone, but also integrated into relationships between all the stakeholders, to build the kind of commitment which the Bath team has been able to demonstrate is essential for better business performance.

The team has, therefore, delved once again into its extensive data pool, created over three years of in-depth qualitative research, to provide some further insights into the nature and impact of vision and values and explore strategies for practitioners to act on the evidence to shape visions and values that will make a difference in their organisations.

Angela Baron
Adviser, Organisation and Resourcing, Chartered Institute of Personnel and Development

Executive summary

- In assessing the connection between people management and organisational performance a focus on HR policy is necessary, but not sufficient. The way line managers implement policy and manage people is vital, but successful companies also have strong values which express beliefs and norms about what is important and about appropriate, valued behaviours.

- If these values are widely shared across the organisation and are reflected in everyday actions of employees at all levels, individually and collectively, then we say there is a strong culture.

- Strong shared-culture companies tend to have better performance, seen in levels of organisational commitment, quit rates, customer satisfaction and appropriate financial measures. Nationwide is a good example of such a company (see Chapter 2) and Chemlab is an example of a much smaller firm where knowledge management is critical. It is a value-driven company (Chapter 3). Values and cultures need to be unique to the organisation, widely shared and relevant to the company purpose and strategy. Dataware (Chapter 3) is an example of value fragmentation in an acquisition-based growth company.

- HR policy, especially in critical areas of recruitment, selection and induction, training and development, performance management and communication and involvement, reflects and reinforces organisational values and culture. It is one of the principal conduits in which and through which culture and values are expressed. Since particular kinds of people are attracted to particular types of organisation, values and culture are a part of employer branding, whether planned or unplanned.

- It is not possible to manage all aspects of organisational culture since much of it is tacit, unexpressed and exists as hidden value assumptions. What organisations can do is to make explicit some key parts of the value construct. Some do this by focussing on a 'Big Idea', something – a few words – which expresses what the purpose or key values of the firm are. The Big Idea is a simple way of expressing some basic assumptions about what the organisation is and how it works, or is meant to work.

◘ The Big Idea is reflected in extensive communications about values and performance and is often part of the Balanced Scorecard. A growing number of companies use extensive measures of employee and customer attitudes and hard measures of performance, integrating them together into a predictive model of the employee–customer profit–chain. HR metrics are of growing importance and one way of measuring the effect of value sharing.

◘ The Big Idea, to be effective, has to be embedded across the whole organisation, integrated with customer/client/patient values of service, built around or upon an enduring legacy of past success, and enacted in behaviour (and thus, not just rhetoric). This behaviour is repeated, collective and routine and is, therefore, habitual.

Chapter 1

◘ **Describes and defines organisational culture and values and emphasises the need for these to be widely shared to be effective.**

◘ **Discusses the role of HR policies and practices as key conduits through which culture and values come to be expressed and realised.**

◘ **Provides evidence to show how strong shared-value companies have higher levels of organisational commitment.**

1 | The importance of vision and culture in people management: theory and evidence

In the search for how human resource management (HRM) impacts on organisational performance many researchers have looked at the types of policies used and their coverage, and linked these to measures of corporate performance like profit or shareholder value. The results have generally been positive, but we have been left with a problem of understanding why such positive associations exist. Our CIPD-funded research (Purcell *et al* 2003, Swart *et al* 2003) in 12 mainly large organisations and six smaller knowledge-intensive firms (see the Appendix for details of these companies) took a different approach by asking employees about their attitudes to work and to specific policies and practices in HRM (and people management more broadly) and the way they were implemented. While we were able to identify 11 core, critical HR policies that were important as far as employees generally were concerned, we placed emphasis on two extra dimensions that made a difference. One was the way line managers, especially front-line managers, implemented and applied these policies and interacted with their teams and employees. They played a critical role in 'bringing policies to life' and in providing local leadership. We reported on this recently in an Executive Briefing (Purcell and Hutchinson 2003).

The second dimension, which we called 'the Big Idea', was the existence in some of the organisations we studied, but by no means all, of a clear sense of mission, underpinned by values, and a culture expressing what the firm is and its relationship with its employees. In some cases this mirrors or echoes the organisation's relationship with its customers. This Executive Briefing explores the Big Idea in more detail, showing why it is important yet elusive, how it affects employees, and how they affect it, what particular HR policies are linked to the Big Idea and what the effects are. We give a number of case histories from among our research companies, draw out some implications for policy and practice and pay particular attention to how some aspects of values can be measured and managed.

First, we need to understand the fundamentals in the link between people management and performance so we can locate the contribution vision, values and culture make. It is necessary to note that what has been termed 'Human Resource

Advantage', or HRA for short, (Boxall 1996) is made up of two linked elements: human capital advantage (HCA) and organisation process advantage (OPA). This comes from the commonsense observation that successful firms are likely to have both better people and better processes. The obvious analogy is with sports teams. HCA is at the heart of standard HRM since it points to excellent recruitment and selection, good training and development, appropriate performance management, effective job and team design that encourages learning and avoids boredom, and workable forms of involvement where skills and knowledge have an avenue for expression and growth. OPA is about the ways work and meaningful activity are organised so that people combine together, and work with technology, to integrate their activities and in dealing with customers, suppliers and responding to competitor threats.

> '...the function of effective people management is to persuade, induce, cajole, or encourage employees to do as good a job as possible...'

It is often hard to describe how precisely these processes happen, why they are done and where they come from. This is where tacit knowledge is important, for example. Researchers often refer to 'path dependency', meaning the strong legacy of history, or to the 'way things are done' – one of the simplest definitions of culture which, like Topsy, 'just growed'. While structures can be designed, behaviours of collaboration or

competition, involvement or control, integration or fragmentation, cooperation or conflict are more difficult to order and change. Some companies have highly successful processes which give them an advantage over their competitors whether competing for economic reward, or resources (as in the public and voluntary sectors). Often this process advantage remains hidden from view, is difficult to unravel and so is hard to copy. It also gives added value in a way that no other resource can do. OPA is therefore central to achieving and maintaining sustained competitive advantage. Organisational values and culture are frequently seen as a key ingredient in OPA.

We need to be clear, too, how this is related to better performance. Before we can explore this in detail it is necessary to reiterate the central proposition in the link between people and performance. Building on the work of American researchers like MacDuffie (1995) and Appelbaum and her colleagues (2000), we show that the function of effective people management is to persuade, induce, cajole, or encourage employees to do as good a job as possible (whether more, or better, or more innovatively) both individually and in working with others. This extra behaviour beyond the minimum can rarely be forced. It has to be given by employees and is therefore discretionary in the sense of 'going the extra mile' or taking responsibility for actions or outcomes that are not strictly part of the job as given in the job description. Organisational effectiveness comes when a significant or large proportion of employees at all levels engage in discretionary behaviour which is valued by the firm and fellow employees. We know from research in the psychological contract and in organisational citizenship behaviour (see Coyle-Shapiro *et al* 2004) that people with high levels of affective commitment to their organisation and to their fellow workers, and who find their work satisfying, are more likely to engage in discretionary behaviour. Thus actions which help generate commitment are central to the people–performance equation.

The classic definition of organisational commitment is the relative strength of an individual's identification with, and involvement in, a particular organisation. It has three attributes:

- ❑ a strong belief in, and an acceptance of, the organisation's goals and values,

- ❑ a willingness to exert considerable effort on behalf of the organisation,

- ❑ a strong desire to maintain membership in the organisation (Porter *et al* 1974).

The importance of vision and culture

If organisational commitment is important as an antecedent to discretionary behaviour we need to be clear how such commitment comes to exist, and what is the contribution of organisational values and culture. We noted in our research how employees who said they had high levels of commitment to their organisation[1] were more

likely to be satisfied, often highly, with HR policies and practices, especially training, career opportunities, job challenge and job influence, performance appraisal, rewards and recognition, efforts to help employees achieve a work–life balance, communication and involvement. Added to these was a strong link to commitment where there was satisfaction with the way line managers applied these policies and the quality of the relationship between them and their work group.

These policies and practices are important in their own right but taken together we can say two further things. First, they are at the heart of the type and range of activities which mould expectations about what opportunities are offered or promised by the employer for personal development, job growth and security, and help establish what is expected of employees in return. As such, policies and practices both reflect and help determine key aspects of the reciprocal exchange between employees and managers. Second, these policies, practices and line manager behaviour both reflect and reinforce (or weaken where they are ineffective) organisational values and, in a broader sense, the culture of the firm. The HR policies and practices are one of the most obvious conduits through which culture and values are expressed or given meaning.

Organisational values and cultures first received prominence in the early 1980s with the publication of *In Search of Excellence* by Peters and Waterman (1982) and *Corporate Cultures* by Deal and Kennedy (1982). The view then was that values were determined by senior management and culture could be designed as something an organisation had or ought to have. Deal and Kennedy showed that successful firms were distinguished from those less successful through their clearly articulated shared norms and values regarding organisational functioning. The emphasis on *shared* norms and values is the key since this draws attention to the distinction, crucial in HR, between espoused and enacted policies. Just as we showed that front-line managers were central to enacting or making policies work, so in studies on culture and values the frequent gap has been noted between what ought to happen and what does happen. It has often been observed that:

repetition by top managers of what is important, or the printing of company values on parchment, does not mean that members of the organisation accept these as important.

O'Reilly and Chapman 1996, p166

> *'...successful firms were distinguished from those less successful through their clearly articulated shared norms and values regarding organisational functioning.'*

This problem of enactment has led researchers and theorists to see culture and values as reflecting organisational life rather than something imposed from the top down by senior management. Thus, it is often argued that culture is something to do with what the organisation 'is', rather than what it just 'has', or has been given by senior management. In this sense culture is hard, if not impossible to manage and manipulate at the whim of top management. If senior management wants to influence organisational culture it needs to be aware of the variety and complexity of existing cultures or culture in the organisation. It is more helpful to identify values and beliefs that are generally and widely shared in the organisation. Senior management can, if it recognises the value of doing so, make these beliefs and values more visible in its communications and especially in its behaviour, and in clearly indicating what it expects of others. Thus O'Reilly and Chapman (*ibid* p160) define culture as 'a system of shared values [that define what is important] and norms that define appropriate attitudes and behaviour for organisational members [how to feel and behave]'. The most famous definition is by Schein:

Organisational culture is the pattern of basic assumptions that a given group has invented, discovered or developed in learning to cope with its problems of external adaptation and internal integration and that have worked well enough to be considered valid and therefore to be taught to new members as the correct way to perceive, think and feel in relation to these problems.

Schein 1985

At the heart of organisational culture are hidden values which are *unconscious, taken for granted beliefs, perceptions, thoughts and feeling which are the ultimate source of values and action.*

Schein 1996

In this sense some part of organisational culture is unmanageable in that it is not capable of being directed, but it means that attempts to articulate and reinforce appropriate values and norms need to reflect these hidden values and build on them in part by making some of these values more accessible. For this reason some studies have argued, and shown in field research, that

shared perceptions of daily practice [are] the core of an organisation's culture

and that

the values of founders and key leaders undoubtedly shape organisational cultures but the way these cultures affect ordinary members is through shared practice.

Hofstede *et al* 1990, p311

This daily practice, the influx of new members as well as new leaders, and changing external challenges and uncertainties mean that culture and organisational values are usually dynamic. Very strong cultures, however, are sometimes seen as too inflexible so a balance is needed between weak cultures which do not reflect or establish common norms and values and strong cultures which can

become introvert. If cultures are created by group members and shaped by key leaders it means they are unique to each organisation. What is viable for one could be disastrous for another. Organisations can emphasise different things. Some may give priority to external performance, others to internal integration. Some are based on the primacy of leadership, others are more egalitarian and collegial and yet others maybe meritocratic or even elitist (Kabanoff *et al* 1995).

'**If cultures are created by group members and shaped by key leaders...they are unique to each organisation. What is viable for one could be disastrous for another.**'

This is very much in tune with the idea that there is no one particular or universal way of managing people in every firm. The need is to find the best fit linking people's needs with those of the competitive or resource position of the firm. Whatever the mission or seeming purpose of the company, for values and culture to contribute to a success they must be broadly shared and consistent (Gordon and DiTomaso 1992, p794), enacted in daily practice and reinforce peoples' desire to contribute and stay with the organisation.

One of the most obvious ways this occurs is through the 'person–organisation fit'. This is seen first in job choice. Particular kinds of individuals are attracted to particular kinds of organisation and those who do not fit soon leave (Sheridan 1992). This is particularly relevant where the 'fit' is to values based on norms and commitment seen in inter-personal relationships, for example, as opposed to instrumental contract compliance. There is clear evidence, certainly among studies on accountants, that retention rates were much higher where this fit was achieved (O'Reilly *et al* 1991).

Two implications flow from this. First, people have to know what sort of organisation would best suit them, thus placing emphasis on employer branding, becoming an employer of choice and simultaneously having or using realistic job previews and forming realistic expectations of the nature of organisational life. Second, organisations are increasingly moving to recruitment and selection techniques based on attitudinal and behavioural profiling and using different ways of screening applicants, often remotely through highly structured telephone interviews.

> *'...careful induction of new employees, the use of buddy systems and supportive team members is important in value reproduction.'*

Interestingly, two of our large companies, both with distinctive cultures and values (Nationwide and Selfridges), had recently adopted this type of selection procedure with excellent results. Some of our smaller knowledge-intensive firms did the same only rather more informally. All were concerned with ensuring a person–organisation fit based around values and 'belonging' and recognised that this was a two-way process. We explore this in Chapters 2 and 3.

What is being looked for is a congruence between individual values and those of the organisation. This may well be at the crux of the person–culture fit. This fit may be to a generalised value such as 'public service' or to a brand like Jaguar and the primacy of quality, or to the dominant profession employed successfully in the firm like software engineering, or to organisational values like 'mutuality' in Nationwide.

Another way of putting this is the search for identity, and these may be multiple – the profession and the organisation. Early experience of work where new members are socialised into prevailing values and culture is crucial in confirming or confounding these shared values (Sheridan 1992). Thus, careful induction of new employees, the use of buddy systems and supportive team members is important in value reproduction. It is here that stories and rituals are learnt and seen to be appropriate in helping to overlay formal controls with social control. Values and culture are a form of social control especially when linked to commitment. When people say they share the values of the organisation they are likely to be expressing a sense of self-fulfilment at work, show an acceptance of appropriate and expected role behaviour and expressing an identification with the firm and often with their occupation or fellow workers, or are identifying with an ideology or wider sense of purpose like 'patient care' or 'public service'. Rousseau (1990) called this 'deep structure identification', beyond the superficial, and showed that this was strongly linked to affective commitment, citizenship and discretionary behaviour.

This, of course, presupposes that organisational values exist in a coherent sense, are known and are enacted or seen in appropriate behaviour. Some of these behaviours will be specific to the organisation in the way it deals with issues such as customer care, handling complaints and reacting to problems and opportunities. Others are more general, reflecting wider societal beliefs about fairness, recognition, support and self-expression. There are often different sub-cultures within organisations. These can be complementary or conflictory. In particular, there may be differences between the executive culture of the top team and that expressed by others, whether the engineers or technocrats who design operating systems, or the people who fulfil the daily work of the organisation: the operators. Schein (1996) notes that

the research findings about the importance of team-work, commitment and involvement fall on deaf executive ears because in executive cultures these are not important values to consider.

Thus, there has to be some congruence between executives and employees in expressing values considered to reflect the purpose and social construction of the organisation and these need to resonate with wider social values that members of the organisation think or see as important. Nationwide's use of the PRIDE initiative is a good example, explored in Chapter 2. The use of employee attitude surveys is growing in

importance and these can be designed to explore values in action as perceived by organisational members. Some questions may relate to general values pertaining in the wider society, such as fairness, opportunity and recognition. Others will reflect values held to be important by senior managers that reflect what is deemed to be important, such as customer service or quality. The use of such surveys on a regular basis gives some opportunity to see how values are shared and, by relating these to performance measures important indicators are obtained and, at times, causal connections established, from attitudes to customer views and performance. The ability to measure and manage values is explored in Chapter 4.

What we termed 'the Big Idea' in the original research report (Purcell *et al* 2003) was the existence of relatively simple values or ideas in some of our research organisations which seemed to express the essence of the firm or organisation in ways which everyone could relate to. Sometimes these were the outcome of careful consideration by the senior management team at a critical moment in the firm's history, as in Nationwide with its emphasis on 'mutuality' (see Chapter 2) and Selfridges, where there was a deliberate attempt to relaunch and expand the store to build on the ideas of the founder, Gordon Selfridge. Before the First World War he had coined the phrase 'everyone is welcome' and this became revamped for 'a store of the 21st century' as 'friendly', to which were added 'accessible', 'bold' and 'aspirational'. At Jaguar, now part of Ford, the word 'quality' was used, but this was not an invention of senior management. It was part of the life of the plant used by unions, employees and managers to indicate the 'essence' of Jaguar in terms of product, processes and people. At Tesco the emphasis was strongly on performance as a performance-driven organisation. As we explore in Chapter 4, these simple Big Ideas become the focus of the balanced scorecard which provides some means to measure and to manage aspects of the Big Idea and underlying values.

> *'the Big Idea...is a simple way of expressing some basic assumptions about what the organisation is and how it works, or is integrated, or co-ordinated.'*

While the Big Idea is not organisational culture, nor the same as organisational values which need to be, and inevitably are, much more nuanced, it is a simple way of expressing some basic assumptions about what the organisation is and how it works, or is integrated, or co-ordinated. To be effective, as we discuss in later chapters, the Big Idea has to be embedded, in the sense of being lived and meaningful, across and throughout the organisation. It has to be enduring, by being historically relevant, building on basic values established over a period, and be about the nature of the organisation and its product or service. It needs to connect or bridge employees and customers, or the inside and the outside of the organisation so that basic values of how customers or suppliers, or patients and clients are treated are not out of line with employee management. Since

the Big Idea is expressive of certain appropriate values and basic assumptions about behaviour and attitudes, if it is embedded, enduring and connects the inside with the outside, it is very likely to be habitual, that is, seen in everyday behaviour, and seen as normal shared practice.

One of the tests of 'strong' organisation cultures is the extent to which there is consistency, by which is meant widespread agreement about the organisation of work, the emphasis on human resources, decision-making processes and co-ordination activities. If consistency is matched with appropriateness the outcome can be powerful.

A strong culture from the standpoint of consistency, and an appropriate culture from the standpoint of content, will [each] produce positive results, but a combination of the two is most powerful.

Gordon and DiTomaso 1992, p794

In summary:

- ◘ Organisational culture is a system of shared values and beliefs about what is important, what behaviours are appropriate and about feelings and relationships internally and externally. Values and cultures are lived and reflected in daily practice. Company values, as articulated by senior management, have to be congruent with these deeper values or culture to be influential.

- HR policies and practices are key conduits which allow these values to be reflected and reinforced, made more accessible and enacted in practice. Thus they are the antecedents of employee behaviour and organisational commitment. The role of line managers is vital here. Taken as a whole these HR practices can be seen as crucial aspects of the employer's part in the psychological contract and in providing organisational support for citizenship behaviour.

- Different organisations have different cultures and values. There is no one best culture, but organisational values need to mesh with wider social values held by stakeholders. At times these may conflict, and each organisation, consciously or unconsciously, will emphasise one over another, eg shareholders, customers, employees, suppliers and the community values. The use of a balanced scorecard is one way some organisations try to manage priorities between stakeholders.

- Particular kinds of people are attracted to particular organisations. This 'person–organisation fit' is most usually related to values, norms and purposes rather than to instrumental values of contract. Thus, there are strong links to higher levels of commitment and better retention when this fit is achieved. This has powerful implications for employer branding, behavioural and attitudinal-based screening of recruits and the active formation of realistic expectations.

- Sub-cultures are an inevitable feature of organisations, especially larger ones, but there has to be an over-arching congruence between executive values as revealed in actions, symbols and rituals, as well as in policies and communication, and those held by other organisational members. In some organisations these can be simply expressed as a Big Idea expressing basic assumptions and norms. For these values to be shared they have to be known, be consistent and reflected in daily practice. Organisations are increasingly looking for ways of finding out how well they are doing this through the use of employee surveys and other types of employee metrics.

> *'For...values to be shared they have to be known, be consistent and reflected in daily practice.'*

Evidence from the People and Performance research

In the course of our research in the period 2000–2003 we interviewed 609 employees at least once in the 12 companies in the People and Performance research. Many of these we interviewed a second time a year later. We used a carefully constructed questionnaire which included questions from a national survey (WERS 1998) to enable us to make comparisons with the wider national picture. We did the same in the knowledge-intensive firms but, given their particular characteristics of smallness and knowledge-based value, we do not include the questionnaire responses here, but in Chapter 3 we report on two of the six companies and the role of values and culture.

Looking particularly at the extent to which employees agreed, or strongly agreed, with the statement 'I share the values of my company', correlational analysis revealed particularly strong associations or linkages with some aspects of HR policy and practice. In particular, there was a strong likelihood that employees would express high levels of identification with the firm's values when:

◘ They were satisfied with the amount of information they received about how well the company was performing, how they contributed to the company achieving its business objects, and believed that everyone in the firm was well aware of the long-term plans and goals of the organisation. Taken together these questions assess the effectiveness of communication.

◘ They were satisfied with methods used to appraise their performance.

◘ They were satisfied with their pay, and their pay compared with others, and with the benefits they received other than pay.

◘ They felt they were provided with good opportunities to express grievances and raise issues of personal concern. We called this 'openness'.

◘ They felt their job was secure.

◘ They felt satisfied with the influence they had in company decisions that affected their job or work. This is a measure of involvement.

◘ They agreed that managers were good at keeping everybody informed about proposed changes, providing everyone with a chance to comment on proposals, responded to suggestions from employees, dealt with problems at the workplace and treated employees fairly. In short, their relationship with their managers was good.

◘ They also had high levels of satisfaction with the amount of influence they had over their job, the sense of achievement they got from their job and the amount of respect they received. This is a measure of job satisfaction.

Less strong, but still significant, associations were found with training, career opportunities, work–life balance and how much effort they made in their job. Taken together these policies and practices constitute an effective HR system which contributes to positive performance. As noted earlier, this mix of HR policy and practice is both a conduit through which values are expressed and enacted and, by their action, express deep-seated shared values.

Looking more closely at the data, we were able to identify six of our 12 companies which seemed to us, as a result of our many visits and discussions

Figure 1 | Employee perceptions of organisation values

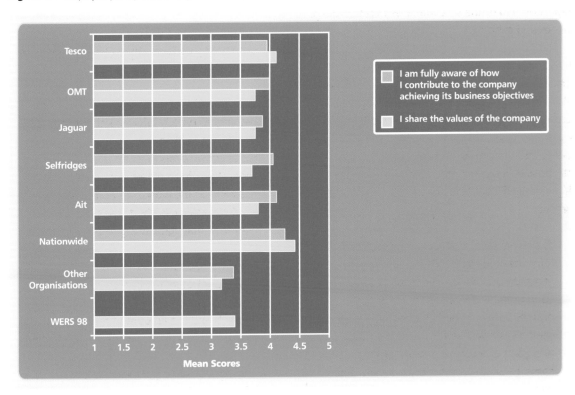

Source: WERC People and Performance Research. N=609

with a wide range of people at all levels in addition to our employees survey, to have strong shared values. In these six strong shared-value organisations, shown in Figure 1, we found that the level of organisational commitment was much higher than in the other six, (the penultimate row on Figure 1) and when compared to the national picture or WERS (the bottom row of Figure 1).

Using more sophisticated statistical techniques of multi-variant analysis, which allow the independent effect of each variable or factor (ie each policy and practice) to be assessed, we are able to show that in strong shared-value companies a particular set of policies were especially effective in allowing us to explain 40 per cent of the causes of organisational commitment.

Figure 2 | Policies associated with organisation commitment in six strong shared-values companies and six weak shared-values companies (rank order)

Strong shared-value companies	Weak shared-value companies
Organisation Commitment (R^2.403)	**Organisation Commitment (R^2.278)**
Drivers: Communication	Drivers: Openness
Relationship with manager	Rewards and recognition
Career opportunities	Communication
Work–life balance support	Effort
Involvement	

Source: WERC People and Performance Research.

In the six companies with weak or fewer shared values, not only was the level of organisational commitment lower but we could only identify 28 per cent of the causes of organisational commitment. This is shown in Figure 2 above.

In summary, levels of organisational commitment are higher in strong shared-value companies and can be explained largely by policies and practices which fit the values, like communications, the way managers manage, the belief that people have in opportunities for career progression and involvement, and the way the organisation tries to help people achieve a satisfactory balance between work and home. In companies with relatively weak shared values, organisational commitment is lower and it is more difficult to identify the drivers of these. The type of practices we can identify are vaguer like 'openness' – the ease of raising problems with your boss – and rewards and recognition, in being how satisfied people are with the way their contribution is recognised. Communication is important but not nearly so strong in its effect as in strong shared-value companies. People who put in a lot of effort also show higher levels of commitment in these weak shared-value companies. Not surprisingly, fewer people in these companies with low levels of shared values are aware of how they contribute to the company achieving its objectives and fewer share the values of the company, as shown in Figure 1. This, of course, requires people to know and understand the business objectives of their company and its values. No wonder communication in all its meanings comes out as such a powerful link to commitment in firms with high levels of shared values and is central to the articulation of values and culture.

Endnote

1   Organisational commitment is measured by asking employees how much they agree or disagree with three statements:

- ◻   I feel proud to tell people who I work for.

- ◻   I feel loyal to my company.

- ◻   I share the values of my company.

Chapter 2

◘ **Discusses the form that the Big Idea takes in Nationwide and consider how this is supported by HR policies.**

◘ **Describes and seeks to explain the links between the values and culture of the society and the performance of the business measured in various ways.**

◘ **Considers the implications of this study for our understanding of the importance of values and culture more generally.**

2 | Values and culture and the link with business performance in Nationwide

This chapter examines the importance of values and culture by drawing on a detailed case study of the Nationwide Building Society. This case not only demonstrates the positive influence of shared, strong values but it also allows us to develop the concept of the Big Idea. We distinguish between 'macro' values held by employees towards senior managers and the organisation as a whole and 'micro' values held towards their local branch office and their immediate line managers. Macro values are especially strong in Nationwide and have a close link with performance, but there is greater variability in the attitudes held towards employees' local working environment.

We first describe the organisational context and the form the Big Idea takes in Nationwide and examine the links between employee attitudes and organisational performance using the concept of HR Advantage discussed in Chapter 1. This is followed by an analysis of the findings and consideration of the implications of our discussion.

Our research in Nationwide began in late 1999 and lasted for three years. We focussed on one part of the business, following extensive interviews at corporate level. More recently, Nationwide has allowed us access to its internally collected data based on branches in the retail network. This has allowed us to engage in a wider analysis of the links between employee attitudes and behaviour, measures of customer satisfaction and financial performance. We use some of this data here. We are very grateful to Nationwide for allowing us to use its data. The interpretation is ours and does not reflect Nationwide policy or views.

> *'Macro values are especially strong in Nationwide and have a close link with performance...'*

Nationwide Building Society: background, values and structure

Established over 150 years ago, Nationwide is one of the UK's largest financial service organisations and provides a broad range of retail financial products and services to over 10 million members including mortgages, savings, current accounts, life assurance, personal loans and household insurance. It is the largest building society in the world and employs around 16,100 staff (13,478 full time employees), the bulk of whom (7,544) work in the network of 681 branches across the country. The remainder are employed in two major offices in Swindon and Northampton and in seven administrative centres.

Mutuality

The Big Idea in Nationwide is derived from its commitment to its mutual status whereby it is owned by its membership rather than shareholders. As building societies have converted to plc status this characteristic of ownership has come to distinguish Nationwide from its competitors and is translated into a set of values which are applied to members and employees alike.

> '...initiatives have emphasised the difference between Nationwide and the banks and...to promote its image as champion of the consumer in the personal financial market.'

Nationwide's stance on mutuality began back in 1995, and resulted in the development of a new business strategy to improve customer services and streamline operations by reducing margins. Various initiatives have emphasised the difference between Nationwide and the banks and, in particular, have promoted its image as champion of the consumer in the personal financial market. The Society recently estimated that over the previous five years members had been better off by £2.7 billion compared to an equivalent plc.[1]

The Big idea: PRIDE

One of the early initiatives in translating 'mutuality' into operational management and associated measures was the use of a form of Key Performance Indicators (KPIs) which are used to measure performance against three key areas.

In 1999 these were expressed as:

- 'Nationwide is my first choice'

- 'Nationwide has the best ratings'

- 'Nationwide is where I want to work'.

Ten KPIs, which all have equal value, are set annually to measure performance against these criteria. Employee satisfaction, for example, (based on the annual employee attitude survey) and competence are used as indicators of 'Nationwide is where I want to work'; mortgage share and complaints are included in measures of 'Nationwide is my first choice'; capital ratios, costs and controls reflect the statement 'Nationwide has the best ratings'. Initially set at corporate level, these measures cascade down into divisional, departmental, team and, finally, individual plans. The KPIs therefore act as a means of communicating the society's values and individuals can see clearly how they influence the corporate objectives. The whole planning process is managed by the Group Planning department which develops the corporate plan (which runs from April to March) after consultation with all divisional directors and the Board. Each division then develops its own plan, with a steer from the Planning department. A traffic light system is used to monitor performance on a monthly basis and progress can be monitored via the Intranet site. All employees receive an annual corporate bonus, which is based on some of the KPIs, and this again can be tracked on the Intranet which provides a quarterly update on the scheme, including examples of how performance has improved and suggestions as to how improvements can be made. This is perceived to be a strong motivational tool.

In the branches targets are set by the divisional director of the branch network, based on targets in the corporate plan. A team bonus is payable based on performance targets and everyone in the team (ie the branch) receives the same amount of bonus, which takes the form of reward vouchers rather than cash. This method is felt to be cost-effective and, according to research, the most popular form of rewarding teams. As one ex-branch manager explained,

the idea is that you can spend it on yourself rather than just using it to pay off a credit card account.

High-performance, league-based competitions are also run under the title of the 'Diamond Club' scheme, rewarding top-performing branches, areas, and individuals on a monthly and annual basis. Branches, for example, compete within the same grade (a branch grading model was introduced in 1995 which is updated every six

months – there are currently five grades), and winners receive a visit from the executive or divisional director, who presents a team plaque or individual award certificate and pin badge. The annual award-winning team(s) also receives some money to pay for a team event of their choosing, while individual winners receive a small prize, such as a weekend theatre break. Details of all the league tables are readily available through a range of media, including the Intranet, staff newsletter, videos, cassettes and noticeboards. Recognition, therefore, rather than financial reward, is clearly a preferred means of motivating staff and more in keeping with the values of the society.

The benefits and obligations of mutuality are stressed for employees. Nationwide seeks to generate a positive set of values and attitudes among its employees that are designed to distinguish them from their competitors and should be reflected in better performance relative to other financial service companies. These values have been summarised in recent years by the PRIDE initiative:

- **P**ut members first

- **R**ise to the challenge

- **I**nspire confidence

- **D**eliver best value

- **E**xceed expectation.

Each year emphasis is placed on one aspect of PRIDE with extensive communications led by the Chief Executive.

'In terms of HRM, Nationwide was rated amongst the best companies to work for, both in the UK and in Europe in 2002, 2003 and 2004.'

In terms of performance outcomes, these have been positive in recent years, seen in regular awards in the financial press, in market share and benefits passed back to members. In terms of HRM, Nationwide was rated among the best companies to work for, both in the UK and in Europe in 2002, 2003 and 2004. In a survey of 1,000 organisations by the European Commission, the society was rated as one of the top 100 best workplaces in the European Union in 2003. It was also rated 11th in the *Financial Times*' '50 Best Workplaces in the UK' in 2003 and 18th in the *Sunday Times*' 'Best Companies to Work For' in 2004. Behind these awards are a wide range of sophisticated HR policies covering all aspects of the employment relationship. These are centrally-determined and applied across all parts of the company, as is commonly the case in retail and financial organisations.

Retail branch network

The retail network is organised into 34 areas each of which includes between 14 and 25 branches. The areas are headed up by an area manager who,

in turn, reports to one of three retail heads of operation, dependent upon location. Each branch offers a broad range of standardised products and services, mortgages, loans, savings and insurance. A typical branch employs around 11 people, including a mix of full- and part-time employees.

HR Function

The HR function at Nationwide is split into three departments: Corporate Personnel, setting strategy and policy; Group Training and Development and Personnel Operations, providing local advice. The employee handbook and all personnel policies and procedures can be freely accessed through the Society's extensive Intranet system. The Intranet also provides briefing notes and guidelines for line managers on a range of HR issues, such as employee development and performance management. In developing and revising its HR policies, Nationwide works closely with its recognised staff association, the NGSU and a high level of partnership working is achieved.

Nationwide has been collecting performance data for many years covering all aspects of the business in line with KPIs. Data comes from operational finance targets such as mortgage conversions and savings, customers are regularly surveyed on the quality of service provision and annual employee surveys are undertaken covering 120 questions (we have combined some of these for this analysis). Response rates are high. In addition, the usual employment data is collected on staff turnover and absence, for example. Data is collected for each branch, but aggregated to an area level to ensure that a more robust statistical analysis is possible.

Employee attitudes and organisational performance

Using this range of data it is possible to explore the interconnection between employee and customer attitudes and performance. There are still relatively few organisations able to undertake this type of analysis. Some of the major employee attitude survey companies claim to be able to do this, but it crucially depends on the organisation collecting a large volume of data across the whole range of operations and integrating these together. We return to this idea of increasing sophistication in HR metrics in Chapter 4.

Here we first consider the evidence relating to organisational performance, measured in different ways and then examine the links between performance and employee attitudes. Our discussion is in terms of the extent to which Nationwide is able to achieve Human Resource Advantage in its various forms, that is, both Human Capital Advantage (HCA) – the policies it adopts, and also Organisational Process Advantage (OPA) – the way those policies are implemented in practice.

Organisational performance

There is clear evidence of a high level of organisational success in Nationwide. The most important measure of financial performance (the percentage value of mortgages sold compared

with the target set) is almost 108 per cent of the target set, although there is quite a high degree of variation around this mean. Measures of customer service are also good, with a mean response of 91 per cent of customers saying they were satisfied or very satisfied with the level of service provided, and 96 per cent saying that the level of service had improved compared with the previous year. Variations around this mean are low, thus showing high levels of consistency typical of strong value companies. The chosen HR measures are also good with low levels of labour turnover (mean $=10.14$ per cent) and absence (mean $=3.56$ per cent).

There are a number of associations between these different measures of performance. As we might expect, sales of mortgages are negatively associated with employee turnover and positively associated with service quality and changes in service quality. Indeed, the association between employee turnover and sales is both large and very significant. The links between sales and service are as we would expect, reflecting the PRIDE mnemonic. Both high employee turnover and absenteeism are associated with lower levels of service quality and changes in service quality. However, we should note that there is no association between absenteeism and the sales of mortgages.

There is strong evidence that Nationwide possesses a Human Resource Advantage. There are high levels of pride among employees (88 per cent) and almost 90 per cent believe the company is a good employer. However, our measures of

Figure 3 | Nationwide correlations between measures of performance and employee attitudes (summarised)

	Mortgages value % *v* target	Employee turnover (% of total FTE)	Employee absence (% of total days)	% customer satisfaction with overall favourable response	% customer satisfaction with service compared to 12 months ago
Mortgages value % *v* target		XX		✓✓	✓
Employee turnover (% of total FTE)	XX				
Employee absence (% of total days)					
% overall favourable response (customer)	✓✓	XX	XX		✓✓
% customer satisfaction with service compared to 12 months ago (customer)	✓		XX	✓✓	
Organisational commitment	✓	XX		✓✓	✓✓
Lagged commitment *	✓	XX		✓✓	
Pay satisfaction	✓	XX		✓✓	✓✓
Team-working				✓	
Openness	✓	XX		✓	✓
Line manager					
Role clarity and understanding contribution		✗		✓✓	

✓✓ correlation significant at the .01 level   ✓ correlation significant at the .05 level

XX negative correlation significant at the .01 level   ✗ negative correlation significant at the .05 level

* Lagged commitment correlates staff commitment in 2002 with performance data one year later

Figure 3 | Nationwide correlations between measures of performance and employee attitudes (summarised) *(continued)*

	Mortgages value % *v* target	Employee turnover (% of total FTE)	Employee absence (% of total days)	% customer satisfaction with overall favourable response	% customer satisfaction with service compared to 12 months ago
Senior management effectiveness	✓	✗		✓✓	✓✓
Job satisfaction				✓✓	✓
Attitude towards recent changes				✓✓	✓
Training				✓✓ .	✓
My last performance review accurately reflected my performance	✓	✗	✗	✓✓	✓✓
Nationwide is good at promoting its best people				✓	

✓✓ correlation significant at the .01 level   ✓ correlation significant at the .05 level
✗✗ negative correlation significant at the .01 level   ✗ negative correlation significant at the .05 level

'organisational commitment' provide the clearest evidence of the existence of HRA because they are likely to be the result of the combination of Human Capital Advantage and Organisational Process Advantage.

Organisational commitment is strongly and positively correlated with mortgage sales, service quality and changes in service quality, and negatively associated with employee turnover (see Figure 3 opposite and above). Sales per full-time equivalent staff are also significantly related to organisation commitment.

In summary, at the general level, there is clear evidence that emphasis on culture and values, seen in the mnemonic PRIDE, with each letter representing a particular aspect of Nationwide values and 'mutuality' is reflected in high levels of organisation commitment. This, in turn, is strongly related to customers having positive views on service quality, better financial performance seen in mortgage values against target, and in rates of labour turnover.

However, when we begin to look beneath the surface the story gets rather more complex. We begin by looking at the evidence of Human Capital Advantage.

Human Capital Advantage: the impact of HR policies and practices.

There are high levels of satisfaction with some policies, including job security (86 per cent saying they believe their job is secure), communication (94 per cent), training (76 per cent), appraisal (76 per cent) and the level of their involvement (77 per cent). There are other, slightly more indirect, indicators of satisfaction with HR policies, including high awareness of how employees contribute to the goals of the organisation and a clear understanding of their job responsibilities. In all these there is strong evidence of high levels of consistency.

However, satisfaction with pay, as is often the case, is somewhat lower. Almost half the staff believe that pay and benefits are better elsewhere, and there is particular dissatisfaction with the level of basic pay. Satisfaction with bonus pay and recognition more generally, is a little higher. There are also concerns with the salary structure: only around two-thirds of employees believe their job

family level accurately reflects their skills and responsibilities. There is more unevenness or lack of consistency in these results. Some people feel satisfied, others do not. Does this matter?

Objectively, based on external comparisons with 160 organisations used by Nationwide to assess pay competitiveness, pay is not particularly out of line and satisfaction scores internally have improved slightly in the recent past. If there were clear evidence of pay being significantly out of line, action could be taken. What is really interesting is that levels of satisfaction with pay are strongly associated with various measures of performance. Figure 3 shows that satisfaction with pay is strongly positively associated with perceptions of service quality and changes in service quality and slightly less strongly associated with mortgage sales. Positive attitudes towards pay are also strongly negatively associated with employee turnover. This does not mean that low pay is the cause of lower levels of customer service and staff turnover. The relationship is more complex, as we noted in our study of Tesco, where identical rates of pay were associated with widely differing views on the adequacy of pay rates. People who are dissatisfied with aspects of working in Nationwide are also, it seems, dissatisfied with their pay, while those on identical rates who enjoy working in Nationwide tend to rate their pay satisfaction higher, and it is these employees who provide good or better customer service. This recalls the discussion in Chapter 1 on the importance of organisational culture in helping to achieve a person–organisation fit.

Two other two key HR policies are of interest: performance appraisal and training, where employee attitudes are somewhat related to performance and customer views. Satisfaction with the accuracy of performance appraisal is linked positively with mortgage sales and the two customer measures of service quality, and negatively associated with both employee turnover and absenteeism. Training is associated with both customer measures of service quality. In other words, there is reasonable evidence to hypothesise that high-quality HR policies in key areas do feed through into higher levels of performance. These polices, as we have argued earlier, are a reflection of wider values. It is also clear that this relationship can operate to the detriment of the company. People dissatisfied with their pay, often as a reflection of wider dissatisfaction, were less likely to show commitment, more likely to leave and not be so good at customer service.

Organisational Process Advantage: processes in people management.

It is helpful to distinguish between two forms of OPA, first, what we refer to as 'macro' OPA, which refers to employee attitudes towards the processes which are essentially common to the whole organisation and are commonly orchestrated from Head Office; and second, 'micro' processes, which are dependent upon the ways in which local managers at branch level are seen to carry out their responsibilities.

At the macro level there is strong evidence of satisfaction with organisational OPA. Employees in Nationwide believe that their senior managers are effective. More than eight out of ten believe that the company is well-managed and senior management have a clear idea of where they are going, and around three-quarters usually believe what they are told by senior managers. These results portray an organisation where there are strong values and underpin the findings about the high levels of organisational commitment. Not only are these values high but, as Figure 3 shows, there is a clear association between senior manager effectiveness and mortgage sales and the two customer measures of service quality.

> '...there are inevitable limits to the power of strong organisational values, even in a company such as Nationwide.'

Once we begin to look for micro-level OPA at the branch level, then we begin to find a much more variable picture, as expected. In part, this may be due to variations in management at the local level, but it will also reflect the environment in which the branch trades. In some, trading is easy. In others, it is real struggle to succeed against the competition. This, of course, means that there are inevitable limits to the power of strong organisational values, even in a company such as Nationwide. There is some strong evidence of OPA at the branch level. On average, around three-quarters of employees believe that their line managers are good at making decisions, tell them what they need to know to do their job, encourage them to create new ideas and act on these suggestions. Similarly, when it comes to team-working, a high percentage (83 per cent) feel members of their team co-operate well to get the work done and that their team is well-led (74 per cent). There are also positive responses in the area of openness, with high proportions of employees believing they can discuss pressures with their manager and work colleagues. There is also evidence of quite high levels of job satisfaction with around three-quarters saying they have sufficient tools and resources to do their job, have opportunities to do it well and the freedom to get on with it.

> *'...around three-quarters...[of employees]...have sufficient tools and resources to do their job, have opportunities to do it well and the freedom to get on with it.'*

There is more variation in other aspects of the line or branch manager role, especially where one-to-one interactions are required. Only just over half of the respondents feel that their manager takes time to coach and develop their on-job skills and around two-thirds feel that their manager helps them to put their formal training and development into practice and that he or she gives them constructive feedback on their performance. A similar number feel it is safe to speak up and challenge the way things are done.

The overall picture of OPA is mixed. There is strong evidence of OPA at the organisational level and some evidence at the branch level. However, there are also areas where there appears to be more variation between managers, especially in dealing one-to-one with employees. This view is confirmed when we look at the links with performance as shown in Figure 3. The strongest links are between the openness construct and mortgage sales, both measures of service quality and employee turnover, with the signs that we have previously found. However, there are no associations between line manager quality and our measures of performance, and team-working has only a weak association with service quality. At first view this is surprising and much further discussion is required in the following section.

Discussion

The overall picture is that performance is strong in Nationwide and there is clear evidence that the HR policies and processes combine in such a way that they support the performance of the business. The associations between organisational commitment and performance are particularly strong. The evidence on HCA is rather more mixed ie, whereas some policies such as training and performance management are clearly positively associated with performance, views on pay systems and structures are different. Here there are lower levels of satisfaction, as is often the case in questions of pay, although the association with performance is still strong. Organisational level OPA is generally very strong and associated with performance but branch level OPA is more variable.

The key question now is how can we explain this pattern of results. There are a variety of factors which might be considered: the external contextual influences, the internal context together with the combination of HR policy and practice.

Nationwide has been operating in a very competitive market during the period under consideration. There have been a number of new entrants into the market and existing players have become much more aggressive. Throughout this time Nationwide has emphasised the principle of mutuality and has stressed that this branding applies equally to customers, products and employees. The PRIDE mnemonic is well-established and understood by employees.

More generally, the organisation is concentrated in the financial services sector and is highly standardised. Its 681 branches are essentially selling the same products and providing common services. This structure lends itself readily to common HR policies and practices and the development of a clear culture and set of values that apply equally to the branch network. Moreover the Head Office is highly visible and frequently referred to. This combination of standardisation and centralisation facilitates the development of a common approach to people management.

This approach is clearly seen when we examine the HR policies themselves. The content of these policies is designed to support the strong culture and values. Recruitment and selection are carefully tuned to these values, and the induction process at branch level lasts for two weeks and is complemented by a buddy system for the first two years. There is also a good bundle of mutually supporting pay and benefits. For example, many employees have access to the final salary pension scheme, there is free health care for around half of employees, a formal agreement on employment security exists and around three-quarters of employees belong to the trade union. The union has recognition for both individual and collective issues, including pay and works in partnership with Nationwide, helping to develop and refine HR policies. One outcome indicator of this rich mix of policies is the relatively high levels of long service of employees: almost two-thirds of employees have been with the company for more than five years, a similar proportion are over 30 and three-quarters of them work full time. This is higher than the average for the sector.

All these policies contribute to the high level of organisational commitment and the development of HRA and especially HCA. However, as we have seen, the development of OPA is rather more mixed, especially at branch level. Understandably there are variations in performance at the local level. Strong central leadership backed by and based on strong corporate values, as in Nationwide, is never enough. It cannot obviate the need for highly effective local management, especially where trading circumstances vary between branches. The use of sophisticated, multi-channel performance and attitudinal data enables companies to identify inevitable weak areas. On the whole there is high level of support of local managers by employees.

Implications

This case has clearly illustrated the close links between organisational commitment and business performance. In particular, it has highlighted the potential positive effect of widely-shared strong organisational values. On closer inspection we have been able to discriminate between the values that employees hold towards the organisation as a whole including its senior managers (macro values) and those held towards line managers at branch level (micro values). While attitudes towards the organisation and senior managers are consistently strong, the micro values were more variable.

Nationwide has been largely successful at the organisational level in eliminating any potential gap between espoused and enacted policies. However, not surprisingly, they have found this more difficult to achieve at the local level where the implementation of the Big Idea and HR policy is in the hands of nearly 700 branch managers. Gaining an HR Advantage depends not only on establishing a clear set of values that constitute the Big Idea and the HR policies which support them, but also on ensuring that line managers live these values on a day-to-day basis.

This leads us back to the importance of the distinction between human capital and organisational process advantage and to the vital role of local managers in 'bringing policies to life', as we reported in an earlier Executive Briefing (Purcell and Hutchinson 2003). While it is relatively easy to establish a set of values and HR policies, it is much more difficult to ensure these are delivered as intended. The success of any policy depends on the employees' daily experience in the workplace. Nationwide has shown that it is able to do this at a corporate level, but, quite understandably, there are more variations at the local level. As one area manager said,

the corporate vision needs to be made personal for each employee.

Ensuring that the Big Idea and its implementation by line managers are mutually reinforcing is difficult in such a large and dispersed organisation, but the possible benefits are very high.

Endnote

1   The success of this strategy is borne out by the latest results that showed pre-tax profits of £188.4million with a 15.7 per cent share of the residential mortgage market.

Chapter 3

◘ Discusses how successful firms achieve fit between HR practice and firm, and professional values.

◘ compares the experiences of two knowledge-intensive organisations in evolving and enacting values.

3 | Vision and values in smaller companies: two cases of knowledge-intensive firms

In this chapter we use two case studies of small-to-medium-sized, knowledge-intensive firms (KIFs) to illustrate how values evolve and develop in different ways. We support the notion that *values* are reflected in the firm's current practices and historical behavioural patterns rather than in written statements of future idealised states (see Chapter 1). Here we pay attention to the impact of knowledge intensity, and knowledge workers in particular, on the formation and embedding of values.

Some of the factors that influence value formation at the firm level[1] include the history of the organisation, growth strategy, nature of ownership, stakeholders in the network and homogeneity of knowledge work. These cases illustrate further that, particularly for knowledge-intensive firms, it is important to develop a degree of congruence between professional values and the values of the firm in order to retain knowledge workers. A further key finding from our research is that successful firms establish a fit between their HR practices, firm values and professional values. That is, the people-management practices tend to originate from professional values and are seldom imported from the outside under the 'best practice' banner. These people-management practices then play a key role in reflecting and reinforcing the values and norms of behaviour considered important.

In the section that follows we briefly introduce the two cases before sketching out how their history, growth patterns and knowledge intensity have influenced the process of value formation. We then examine the nature of shared values in the firm by developing a framework for value formation, value evolution and value congruence. Finally, we explore the issue of espoused values and whether there is a gap between espoused and enacted values.

It is important to note that at the time of our research neither of the firms had a written set of values that were published in corporate documentation or marketing information. Our findings here reflect that the 'way in which firm values were lived and expressed' by leaders (through their management practices) and knowledge workers (through their behavioural routines) is more significant than written statements of idealised values. Furthermore, the particular question in our research interviews which addressed 'the extent to which values of the organisation were shared' was answered by referring to shared professional values. It is for this reason that the notion of value congruence (the fit between professional values and firm values) is important in our discussion.

The two cases, which illustrate different ways in which the values evolve and are enacted, are Chemlab, a life science research organisation and Dataware[2], a world-leader in e-Publishing Services and Web delivery in the academic and professional sectors. Brief details of the cases are given here and a more detailed discussion can be found in Swart, *et al* (2003).

Chemlab

Chemlab, with 60 employees, is a specialist chemical company with experience in the synthesis of a wide variety of compounds which are often complex, biologically active, molecules. This KIF employs teams of skilled chemists (mainly at post-doctoral level) and operates from one site in the UK and one site in the USA. The organisation is still owned by professional chemists who understand and exemplify professional values held in this research community.

> *'Chemlab is more interested in attracting talented research chemists over a period of time than growing at a fast rate.'*

The business is cash-rich with no funds owing to venture capitalists. It continues to recruit and work closely with universities in order to identify suitable talent. Chemlab is more interested in attracting talented research chemists over a period of time than growing at a fast rate. This enabled the firm to do two important things that relate to value formation: first, it was able to continue to focus on interesting work, rather than following a mass-production strategy, thereby attracting professionals who held similar values to current employees. Second, the process of socialisation into organisational values was simplified as there was one dominant value-set which newcomers from universities were already familiar with. Thus, 'taken for granted' assumptions about the necessity and desirability of a research culture were imported by the owners from their university experience. This strongly influenced the choice of work and made the person–organisation fit easier to attain.

Most formalised HR practices originated from an elaborate HR policy, which was written by the part-time HR manager. She joined the organisation three years prior to our research after she consulted to Chemlab on employee-related matters. During our interviews we seemed to hear two versions of HR practices: those prescribed in the employee handbook and those practised on a day-to-day basis by the employees and managers.

For all concerned, the most important set of practices were those that were related to the performance appraisal. This is due to the fact that it is very difficult to appraise the outcome of research, yet performance evaluation is critical for individuals and the organisation. The performance management processes which were originally designed by the part-time HR manager were subsequently shaped to reflect the nature of research as well as the professional values held by the community of researchers.

A formalised mentoring system was also in place to enhance skills development, although this appeared to operate mainly in the chemistry division. Within this system a mentor is assigned for new employees who will then work very closely with the mentor for up to one year. It was felt that the academic culture accounted for a lot of the coaching given where employees regard it as important to have the opportunity to learn from more experienced staff. Furthermore, the nature of the knowledge is very complex and cannot be passed on easily. One senior manager noted that:

Integration is achieved by getting new, green recruits to work with experienced chemists – this is how they [new staff] get used to the 'ways of the company'. That is why we recruit straight out of academia and grow the commercial experience here.

Formal reward structures reinforce the organisational culture. Team recognition is also related to strengthening the family culture in the form of taking a team out to a meal (recognition) if a job was well done/finished on time. Individual token rewards are also given for outstanding performance. Significantly, most employees felt that the rewards

were generated from the work itself, ie doing a good job as a chemist. This is evidence of the strong professional values within the firm.

Dataware

The three core services that Dataware provides comprise: publisher services (online publishing platform), e-communities (creating content-rich vertical portals) and a search facility (deep web content). Within these three core areas its mission is to be the dominant web intermediary for professional and academic research. The organisation's vision of growth is coupled with the idea of 'bigness': the company wants to create a flourishing market and occupy a dominant position therein in the shortest possible timespan.

> *'…[Dataware] wants to create a flourishing market and occupy a dominant position therein in the shortest possible timespan.'*

This medium-sized KIF is a world-leader in e-Publishing Services and Web delivery in the academic and professional sector. It has substantial venture capital funding and has offices in the UK (Bath and Oxford), and US (Providence, RI and Boston, MA). The company started from a University Computer Services Department in 1998 and was then commercially brought to life by its owner. Since then Dataware has grown both organically and through acquisition: an information architecture firm (US) and one competitor (US paper-based provision of journal searches) were acquired. At the time of our research, Dataware had 200 employees across a variety of specialised areas including: software engineers, software developers, sales executives, producers, project managers, information architects, visual designers, web developers and account managers.

It is not uncommon for the various groups of knowledge workers to be recruited from different clients. This meant that contrasting sets of professional values were held by groups of knowledge workers. The sub-sets of values could also be traced back to that of the client, which meant that there was value congruence across the network (between the firm and the client) but that values were fragmented and not strongly shared within the firm.

> *'...research participants [at Dataware] felt that internal pay-equity was difficult to maintain due to the acquisition of organisations with differing pay systems.'*

Dataware's clients include universities, publishers, libraries and scientific interest groups. A detailed process is followed to retain and capitalise client information. Only key members of staff deal with the client and they follow a specific process of client-contact/proposal development. Every effort is made to maintain client continuity throughout the process, thereby positioning the customer as central to their value-chain.

Dataware does not have a specialist HR function and HR is administered by staff that support the Chief Financial Officer (CFO): records of recruitment, personnel files and salary administration are housed here. The CFO viewed the greatest HR challenges in the face of acquisitions and growth in largely administrative terms such as: the establishment of an HR data base, the refinement of the employment contract, the integration of pay systems and the implementation of the appraisal process. There is heavy reliance on an external HR consultant for the formulation of HR policies and the facilitation of HR. Project team leaders are responsible for the day-to-day implementation of HR practices and their roles include: recruitment needs, identification and interviewing, induction, basic HR administration (records of holidays of team members) and the appraisal of performance.

Each team also has a technical lead who is responsible for technical skills development. Team leaders and technical leads give input into suggested salary increases via the remuneration committee, and overall responsibility for remuneration rests with the CFO. Our research participants felt that internal pay-equity was difficult to maintain due to the acquisition of organisations with differing pay systems. Although Dataware conducted an external pay benchmarking exercise through a consultant, it was believed that 'the matching of roles' with the industry appeared to be particularly tricky due to the depth of roles that existed within Dataware.

Value formation and congruence: comparing the two cases

A comparison of our two case studies highlights the different ways in which values can be developed and enacted in small-to-medium knowledge-intensive firms. For both these firms the issue of value congruence is of particular importance, given that it will influence the retention of knowledge workers. However, differences in history and ownership, growth strategy, nature of the workforce, value socialisation and network relationships influence how strongly values are shared and the extent to which they shape HR practices (see Table 1 on page 34 for a summary of these differences).

Chemlab has taken considerable care to retain a research culture which fits the university departments from which they recruit as well as their clients. Their 'slow growth' strategy has further enabled them to retain the family feel which their employees are proud of. The prevalence of a culture that values professional research has been made possible by the presence of owner/managers who are themselves research scientists, which is an example of how senior managers enact and are concurrently role models of organisational values. Dataware, on the other hand, while it grew from a similar university research culture, has an ambitious growth strategy which relies on acquisitions where values and culture vary and are difficult to integrate. This strategy is influenced by venture capitalists and has led to a fragmented value-set with several sub-cultures each believing in different 'Big Ideas'. There is no over-arching integrative set of values, and few senior managers saw the need for one.

Dataware's fast growth through acquisitions, together with a recruitment strategy which is focused on drawing talent from clients, has resulted in fragmented sets of values within the organisation but shared values across the network. A knowledge worker could be in a position where he or she identifies more with the publisher they worked for previously, for example, than with his or her current employer. This also meant that it was difficult to achieve a person–organisation value fit because, first, the values themselves were fragmented, and second, there was no one dominant set of professional values that could shape the organisational values. If, however, the firm had adopted a growth strategy that allowed for interesting work, they could have addressed a dominant professional value that centred around skill-development.

> '...not only did employees [at Chemlab] feel that they were working with like-minded people, but they expressed strongly that they knew they were building their professional careers.'

On the other hand, maintaining and attracting interesting and challenging work was central to Chemlab's growth strategy. This allowed them to attract knowledge workers who shared the same value-set but, more importantly, they were able to match their organisational value-set to that of the

Table 1 | A comparison of two cases

Value Factor	Chemlab	Dataware
History	Grown from university research departments.	Grown from a university department as well as acquisition of firms who offer related services.
Ownership	Owned by professional chemists.	Venture capital.
Growth strategy	Remain small, focus on family culture and interesting work.	Fast growth, Acquired firms. Moved from bespoke to product-driven strategy.
Homogeneity of knowledge workers	Homogeneous, recruited from specified university pools and employees are retained through the strong organisational culture.	Several different groups of knowledge workers. Strengthened by acquisitions and split between software engineers and software developers.
Attention paid to values	Although the values were not explicit, there was a clear focus on values during recruitment, appraisal, development and reward. Practices were value-driven.	Less attention paid to values at the expense of growth strategy. More a case of best-practice than value-led practices.
Socialisation of values	Small teams with fluid boundaries. Similar age and background of employees allowed for social structures to exist outside the workplace.	Large fragmented teams. Feelings of isolation. Management seemed to be removed from employees. Limited opportunities to develop and maintain firm level values.
Stakeholders in the network	Universities Pharmaceutical firms Patent lawyers Regulatory bodies Suppliers.	Venture Capitalists Publishers Universities Libraries Authors Scientific interest groups.
Evolution of HR practices	Initially from the outside with a subsequent space that is created wherein professionals challenge what could be known as 'best practice' to develop their own sets of practices that fit the set of professional values.	Mainly HR administration. Fragmented practices. Limited contact between employees and external consultant. Project leader responsible for implementation of HR practices, which leads to further fragmentation.

Table 1 | A comparison of two cases *(continued)*

Value Factor	Chemlab	Dataware
Recruitment and selection	Value-driven. Informally through networks which share professional values.	Sub-sets of knowledge workers. Original group from a university. Subsequent recruitment often from clients.
Training and development	Mainly informal through mentoring – which is a prominent vehicle for expressing values.	Limited mentoring. Little training.
Performance management	Redesigned to express and maintain professional values.	Implemented and influenced by project leads.
Pay and reward	Recognition given for maintaining cultural values. Financial rewards for 'doing the job in the right way'. Encouragement for creating a research culture.	Dissatisfaction with pay equity due to integration of several pay systems.
Career opportunities	Influenced by knowledge workers.	*'A career [in Dataware] is something that lasts between today and tomorrow.'*
Job challenge	Challenging work akin to professional values.	*'A job in McDonald's would be slightly more satisfying.'*
Communication	Integral to family culture.	Feeling isolated and removed from management decisions.
Involvement and participation	Several committees that make a difference. Feeling of being involved. Ability to change and influence practices.	Limited opportunity to participate in decision-making.
Value characteristics	Strongly-shared. Evolves from professional values. Drives HR practices. Placed above a fast growth strategy.	Fragmented. Lack of congruence between professional and organisational values. Dictated by the team. Shared values are sacrificed for speed of growth.

professionals who worked for them. That is, not only did employees feel that they were working with like-minded people, but they expressed strongly that they knew they were building their professional careers. The ability to build this collective identity ensured that Chemlab could retain their key knowledge workers.

The strongly-shared professional values in Chemlab also shaped the way in which knowledge workers were managed. This illustrates that not only are people management practices the vehicles through which culture is expressed, but they are also indicators of the degree of value congruence. The sets of HR practices were similar to other professional firms: they allowed high degrees of autonomy, focused on skill development and presented several opportunities for involvement and participation. However, this expression of value congruence was found in pockets in Dataware, and it was clearly a function of the values and management style of the specific project lead.

> *'...the process of mentoring is also a powerful way of keeping organisational values alive and for preserving organisational stories that express the culture.'*

It is important to understand specifically how HR practices are shaped because this is an indicator of professional–organisational value congruence. In Chemlab a set of formal HR policies were developed by a part-time HR manager. However, these written policies served as a framework within which research chemists could challenge practices and design new processes which reflected their values. This process was made possible by the homogeneity of the knowledge workers (a dominant set of values), the fact that the owners themselves shared this professional value-base (they were chemists), and that the culture was built upon involvement and participation (family feel). These factors were not present in Dataware, where knowledge workers were not all that clear about what the 'prescribed' HR practices were. This resulted in high degrees of variation between project teams and indeed professional value-bases. Critically, HR practices were value-led in Chemlab, but in Dataware they were growth-driven.

The way in which values were kept alive also differed greatly between our two organisations. This was particularly evident in their approaches to training and development, their work organisation and the degree of socialisation outside work. In Chemlab it was clear that mentoring was taken seriously. This was also seen as the main vehicle for development. The formal reason given for this approach was that tacit knowledge is central to the success of a chemist and that theoretical knowledge is not enough to be really good at your job. However, the process of mentoring is also a powerful way of keeping organisational values alive and for preserving organisational stories that express the culture. Mentoring in Dataware was something that took place across the network as much as within the organisation. Knowledge workers also commented here that they had limited opportunities to learn from others.

Knowledge-sharing across projects was important to Chemlab, not least because they could 'sell' their knowledge in the networks within which they operated. Their team structures were, therefore, fluid, which aided knowledge-sharing and concurrently ensured that values were not shared just on a team level. Dataware's teams were very large and our research participants remarked that they seldom had the opportunity to know what others were doing or what management was deciding. In a sense the vehicles for value formation and sharing were absent.

This fragmentation was also evident in the 'lack of a feeling of belonging' and employees in Dataware were not rewarded for organising social events. However, Chemlab gave small financial rewards for contribution to the 'family feel'. For example, there was recognition given for the organisation of the festive season function held. Chemlab's social structures also extended beyond the boundaries of the organisation and employees would often meet socially after work. The homogeneity of the workforce enabled these processes of the 'sharing of values' to be kept alive in the organisation.

What we see from these two firms is that the professional–organisational value congruence and the strength of shared values are mutually reinforcing. That is, if an organisation can recruit employees who have strong professional values and if they can shape their organisational values accordingly, then they are likely to retain their key knowledge workers and be able to establish a collective sense of shared values.

Several factors influence this mutually reinforcing capability, ie the history and ownership of the firm, growth strategy, stakeholders in the network, homogeneity of the workforce and structures that enable the socialisation of values. Finally, it is important to understand how people management practices evolved, given that they are not only vehicles through which the culture and underlying values of the organisation are expressed, but their evolution is an indication of the extent to which professional values can shape organisational practices.

Endnotes

1   We differentiate here between professional values, held by a group of employees, and firm level values, held by members of the firm. We argue that the latter is acknowledged at the collective level, even if these values are not accepted, or are challenged verbally or behaviourally. That is, for a dimension of the organisational culture to be regarded as an organisational value (Schein, 1996), it needs to be known or felt and enacted by a majority of the employees, even if it is not written down or formally recorded in company documentation.

2   It has been necessary to use pseudonyms for these two companies to maintain confidentiality agreements made with them at the time of the field work.

Chapter 4

◘ **Discusses the concept of the 'Big Idea' and the attributes which make it effective as a source of organisational commitment.**

◘ **Examines strategies for measuring and managing vision and values.**

4 | Implications for HR policy and practice: measuring and managing vision and values

In a study of employee attitudes in a New York-based bank, Bartel and her colleagues concluded that:

Employee attitudes differ significantly across branches in ways that cannot be explained by branches randomly drawing workers from a distribution of workers with different innate attitudes. Newly-hired workers adopt the favourable or unfavourable attitudes that the branches exhibited before they arrived. Moreover, branches with less favourable attitudes have higher turnover rates, lower levels of sales and lower rates of sales growth than where workers have more positive attitudes.

Bartel et al 2004, p 24.

Our analysis of Nationwide is similar, and in an earlier report we showed marked variations in attitudes and performance in four Tesco stores (Purcell *et al* 2003). In these companies, with extensive, yet centralised, HR policies, variations in attitudes and performance are explained by reference to variance in local management leadership in the context of trading circumstances,

and by the existence of organisational culture – in these cases sub-cultures at branch or store level. The fact that the Bartel study confirmed earlier research on group socialisation – new staff adopt the attitude mix of pre-existing staff – is indicative of powerful group social forces. That these then link to performance is especially interesting and of policy relevance. It confirms the so called 'service–profit chain' (Heskett *et al* 1997), in which companies that provide high quality service, have highly satisfied and loyal customers, satisfied and loyal employees and higher revenue growth.

> **'...companies that provide high quality service, have highly satisfied and loyal customers, satisfied and loyal employees and higher revenue growth.'**

This, and subsequent work in validating these relationships in Sears, where a causal chain exists from positive employee attitudes, through customer retention and spending to profits (Rucci *et al* 1998), are having a profound impact on HR metrics and further sophistication of the balanced scorecard. Nationwide is a good example of how the integration of operational, financial, customer and employee data can be used to provide a sophisticated level of analysis on attributes of performance variation, allowing for better fine-tuned policy interventions. In the process, the HR function becomes increasingly active in, and part responsible for, organisational effectiveness.

The implication is that employee attitudes do matter and these reflect, in part, organisational culture and values. Thus, measuring employee attitudes has become a much more important feature of the HR toolkit, and needs to be integrated with measures of customers' views, and those of suppliers and other stakeholders. It is interesting to note that a survey of firms listed in the 100 best places to work (as Nationwide is) found that employees in those companies had more positive attitudes than employees in a matched sample of companies, and better financial performance (Fulmer *et al* 2002). We can confidently assert that these companies are very likely to have a strong culture (seen in a high level of consistency of agreement among participants) and with an appropriate content for their purposes (ie vision and values must be appropriate for the fundamental aim of the firm).

> *'Culture and values provide the basic parameters for specific policy development without which they can remain generalised wish lists of "good practice".'*

Thus, as we showed in Chapters 2 and 3, there exists in Nationwide, and in a different context in Chemlab, a system of shared values and beliefs

about what is important in and for the company, what behaviours are appropriate (and what are inappropriate) and about feelings and relationships, for example, toward customers and fellow workers.

In these firms there will be an extensive use of HR polices and practices since these are the key conduits that allow vision and values to be reflected and reinforced in daily practice – for example, in recruitment and selection to achieve the person–organisation fit, in performance management to define what is meant by effective performance and individual responsibility for it, in training and development to provide opportunities for relevant skill and competence growth, and in communication and involvement to provide priorities for action, information and participation. Culture and values provide the basic parameters for specific policy development without which they can remain generalised wish lists of 'good practice'.

We noted in our study of 18 companies in our two research projects on People and Performance for the CIPD that some seemed able to capitalise on pre-existing modes of behaviour or aspirations (as in 'quality' in Jaguar or 'excellence' in OMT) to capture the essence of the firm as a Big Idea. This could be formally decided, usually at a crucial period in the firm's life, like 'mutuality' in Nationwide, or it could be emergent as a taken-for-granted assumption, as in Chemlab. The 'Big Idea', to be effective, has a number of attributes:

◘ It needs to be *embedded* across the organisation and widely understood or referred to, not as part of a learnt script but as a reflection of everyday life in the organisation. This is why, in our study of strong shared-value companies, communication came out as so important in employees' perceptions of HR policy. Most employees were able to say that they shared the values of the company.

◘ It is nearly always *integrated* or interconnected with customer-facing values or those relating to the desired relationship with clients, patients or other external stakeholders. While cultural perceptions of a company or organisation can vary between those held inside by employees and those on the outside by customers, in strong shared-value organisations there is a base of societal values like honesty, fairness, respect etc which apply to both. Since employees are themselves consumers, failure to apply standards from one domain to another can cause commitment to the firm to fall.

◘ Values need to be *enduring*. The strong shared-value companies in our sample had built their Big Idea, consciously or unconsciously, on a legacy that allowed people to respond to the idealised values of the past while reflecting present and future states. By being built on the historic values of the organisation they were more likely to be seen as relevant and appropriate. Thus, 'mutuality' goes back to the origins of the building society movement; 'quality' is the very essence of the Jaguar

marque; 'have fun and make money', the values often referred to in AIT (a financial software company), reflected both the industry and the need for innovation and entrepreneurship. 'Friendly, bold, accessible and aspirational', Selfridges' values, had their origin in the values expressed by the founder of the firm 100 years ago.

> *'...in strong shared-value organisations there is a base of societal values like honesty, fairness, respect etc...'*

◘ The implication of studies of organisational culture, vision and values is that sensible firms build on what they have, what is sometimes called 'social architecture'. Senior managers know they cannot dictate what culture their firm should have but they can influence it, for example, in the way HR policies are designed and the importance attached to their effective implementation. Since values, to be meaningful, must influence behaviour, firms with strong shared values tend to have *habitual, collective or routine patterns of behaviour* expressed in everyday life. These relate to interactions between people and norms of conduct and to accepted definitions of wider responsibilities and priorities seen in organisational citizenship behaviour and expressed in organisational commitment.

◘ While many aspects of organisational culture are hidden, tacit and intangible, organisations have increasingly sought ways to *measure and manage* aspects of their Big Idea. The growing sophistication of attitude surveys and the regular collection of marketing, operational, financial and HR metrics and an ability to integrate their interpretation has allowed much deeper understanding of the value of 'values' in influencing productive behaviour.

Measured and Managed

One of the key attributes of the 'Big Idea' as one aspect or organisational culture, is that it can be measured and managed. This means measuring performance in all key aspects of the business, including operational, customer and people issues, as well as the traditional financial performance objectives, such as dividend yield, price to earnings ratio, and return on sales and investment. This helps implement the concept of the 'Big Idea' and also provides a means of integrating different functional areas and decisions into linked processes. Integration can be both vertical, ie linking the top to the bottom – and horizontal, ie interconnecting HR with marketing and finance etc. All six of the organisations with 'strong values', shown in Figure 1 on page 11, had adopted means of measuring the Big Idea, and some of the other organisations had recently introduced measurement initiatives as a means of improving overall performance. This most common approach was through the balanced scorecard or some similar methodology.

Balanced scorecard

The balanced scorecard (BSC), developed by Kaplan and Norton, is one of the most widely known performance measurement systems that helps translate an organisation's values and strategy into measurable objectives across all levels of the organisation. This approach looks at the business from a number of important perspectives and provides answers to some basic questions:

◻ Customer perspective (how do customers see us?)

◻ Internal or process perspective (what must we excel at?)

◻ Innovation and learning perspective (can we continue to improve and create value?)

◻ Financial perspective (How do we look to shareholders?)

Kaplan and Norton, 1992

An integrated mixture of measures are therefore needed which reflect the goals contained in the organisations vision and values. As Kaplan and Norton explain

[senior executives] recognise that no single measure can provide a clear performance target or focus attention on the critical areas of business.

Managers want a balanced presentation of both financial and operational measures.

Kaplan and Norton, 1992

The integrated nature of the approach allows managers to view performance indicators in several areas simultaneously and understand how changes in one area can impact on another. For example, improved financial results achieved through redundancies could adversely affect employee motivation and commitment. By combining different measurements managers can gain a better understanding of the many interrelationships and this can help break down functional barriers.

Tesco

Tesco is an example an organisation which has used the BSC approach to help bring about major cultural change. In the mid 1990s, Tesco sought to develop a customer-facing culture and, to facilitate this, developed their own version of the BSC, converting it into a 'steering wheel', which comprised four quadrants – people, finance, customers and operations. Each quadrant has a number of objectives with clearly defined measures. The people quadrant for example includes the following:

Objectives:	*Example of measures*:
Recruit the best:	% of successful positions filled
Develop people to be the best:	Performance reviews completed
Retain the best:	Absenteeism, staff turnover reducing
Live the values:	% of people who believe that values are practised; job satisfaction

The measures are updated each quarter and link to corporate measures that underpin the organisation's strategic objectives. Each store and many head office functional areas have their own steering wheel that tracks performance on a weekly basis using a traffic light system (red, green, amber) to monitor performance. As one senior head office manager explained, '*the steering wheel holds the business together*', creating a greater focus on people and customer issues, taking the emphasis away from financial and operational results, which had previously driven the organisation.

PricewaterhouseCoopers

PricewaterhouseCoopers introduced the BSC approach in order to ease the merger between Price Waterhouse and Coopers & Lybrand in 1998 –organisations which had very different cultures. The BSC is used in the Assurance and Business Advisory services (ABAS) to set individual and regional performance objectives against the group's objectives which, in 2000, were represented by the acronym ASPIRE, based around three key areas – clients, people and the firm:

A –Assurance and advisory methodology (Clients)

S – Specialisation of our people (People)

P – People retention, recruitment, mobility and development (People)

I – Improvement in revenue and recovery rate (Firm)

R – Risk management and quality (Firm)

E – Exceed client expectations (Client)

Senior managers and managers receive bonuses based on the performance measures.

Selfridges

Selfridges, another organisation with strong values, and described in more detail in our earlier report (Purcell *et al* 2003), has a variety of ways of measuring and managing values. Here the values were expressed in a more articulated form under four goals:

Selfridges should be aspirational, friendly, accessible and bold.

These goals were, in turn, translated into statements so that all stakeholders (employees, customers, shareholders, suppliers and the community) could clearly understand what this meant for them. For example, the value 'bold' was translated into the following:

Employee values:	How does this make me want to work here?
Customer values:	How am I encouraged to shop?
Community values:	How does Selfridges reflect the spirit of the city?
Shareholder values:	Why should we invest in the store?
Supplier values:	What makes Selfridges an interesting proposition?

These are then translated into types of expected behaviours that can be tested in subsequent surveys and inform performance management. Thus, for employees, 'bold' is linked to employee retention (see above) and with hoped-for employee responses, such as 'everyone is passionate about what they do – it energises me', 'we aim to do things better' and 'I am encouraged to step outside the box'. In addition, each department has Key Performance Indicators (KPIs) which include performance measures in relation to profit per square foot, data on 'foot-fall' etc. This information is made available down to the lowest levels through regular team briefings in order to enhance employees' understanding of the business performance, its strategy and values.

In Chapter Two we showed how Nationwide used the BSC effectively and how its sophisticated use of HR metrics aided interpretation of data and an understanding of the drivers of performance. Most importantly, what Nationwide found, and what these other organisations with strong shared values that we studied realised, was that employee values do matter, do vary between, and within, multi-site organisations, and are a reflection of deeper organisational culture and values.

By looking at the link between people management and organisational performance, we have shown in this research that key HR policies, if appreciated by employees, are linked to higher levels of organisational commitment and thus to discretionary behaviour and performance. One crucial feature has been the way line managers, especially those on the front line, apply polices and 'bring them to life'. Underpinning both this positive line manager behaviour and the design and application of HR policies is some sense of what the organisation is, what it is trying to achieve, and what behaviours are valued and appropriate. This vision and value, this notion of organisation culture, while hard to define and grasp, is the foundation of an effective HR system contributing to employee well-being and organisation performance.

Appendix | The research companies

We are very grateful to the managers and employees of these companies for allowing us to undertake our research in the period 2000-2003. Their helpfulness, cooperation and enthusiasm for the research, and openness in being willing to share results, is much appreciated.

People and Performance research

AIT

Clerical Medical

Contact 24

Jaguar

Nationwide Building Society

Oxford Magnetic Technology

PricewaterhouseCoopers

The Royal Mint

Royal United Hospital, Bath

Siemens Medical Solutions

Selfridges & Co

Tesco

People and Performance in medium-sized knowledge-intensive firms

Epinet Communications

Ingenta

Marlborough Stirling

Microgen-Kaisha

MPC Data

Tocris Cookson

We also wish to thank Kostas Tasoulis for help with the literature review in Chapter 1 and Konstantinos Georgiades for his statistical analysis.

References

Appelbaum, E., Bailey, T., Berg, P. and Kalleberg, A. (2000)

Manufacturing Advantage. Ithaca, Economic Policy Institute, Cornell University.

Bartel, A. (2004)

'Human Resource Management and Organizational Performance: evidence from retail banking', *Industrial and Labor Relations Review*.

Bartel, A., Freeman, R., Ichiniowski, C. and Kleiner, M. (2004)

'Can a Work Organisation Have an Attitude Problem? The impact of workplaces on employee attitudes and economic outcomes', *CEP Discussion Paper No 636*. London, Centre for Economic Performance, LSE.

Boxall, P. (1996)

'The strategic HRM debate and the resource-based view of the firm', *Human Resource Management Journal*, 6 (3), 59–75.

Coyle-Shapiro, J., Kessler, I. and Purcell, J. (2004)

'Reciprocity or "It's my job"?: exploring organizationally directed citizenship behaviour in a National Health Service setting', *Journal of Management Studies*, 41 (1), 85–105.

Deal, T. and Kennedy, A. (1982)

Corporate Cultures. Reading, Mass., Addison-Wesley.

Fulmer, I., Gerhart, B and Scott, K. (2003)

'Are the 100 Best Better? An empirical investigation of the relationship between being a "great place to work" and firm performance.' *Personnel Psychology*, 56, 965–993.

Gordon, G. and DiTomaso, N. (1992)

'Predicting Corporate Performance from Organisational Culture', *Journal of Management Studies*, 26 (6), 783–798.

Heskett, J., Sasser, W. and Schlesinger, A. (1997)

The Service Profit Chain. New York, The Free Press.

Hofstede, G., Neuijen, B., Ohayu, D. and Sanders, G. (1990)

'Measuring organizational cultures: a qualitative and quantitative study across twenty cases, *Administrative Science Quarterly*, 35, 286–316.

Kabanoff, B., Waldersee, R. and Cohen, M. (1995)

'Espoused values and organizational change themes', *Academy of Management Journal*, 38 (4), 1075–1104.

Kaplan, R and Norton, D. (1996)

The Balanced Scorecard: Translating Strategy into Action. Boston, MA. Harvard Business School Press.

MacDuffie, J.P. (1995)

'Human resource bundles and manufacturing performance: organizational logic and flexible production systems in the world auto industry', *Industrial and Labor Relations Review*, 48 (2), 197–221.

O'Reilly, C., Chapman, J. and Caldwell, D. (1991)

'People and organizational culture: a profile comparison approach to assessing person–organization fit', *Academy of Management Journal*, 14 (3), 487–516.

O'Reilly, C. and Chatman, J. (1996)

'Culture as social control: corporations, culture and commitment' *Research in Organizational Behaviour*, 18, 157–200.

Peters, T. and Waterman, R. (1982)

In Search of Excellence, Lessons from America's Best Run Companies. New York, Harper and Row.

Porter, L., Steers, R., Mowday, R. and Boulian, P. (1974)

'Organisational Commitment, job satisfaction and turnover among psychiatric technicians', *Journal of Applied Psychology*, 59, 603–9.

Purcell, J., Kinnie, N., Hutchinson, S., Rayton, B. and Swart, J. (2003)

Understanding the People and Performance Link. CIPD, London.

Purcell, J. and Hutchinson, S. (2003)

Bringing Policies to Life: The vital role of front line managers in people management. CIPD, London.

Rousseau, D. (1990)

'Assessing organizational culture: the case of multiple methods', in B.Schneider (ed), *Organizational climate and culture* (153–192). San Francisco, Jossey-Bass.

Rucci, A., Kirn, S. and Quinn, R. (1998)

'The employee-customer-profit chain at Sears', *Harvard Business Review*, 76(1), 82–97.

Schein, E. (1985)

Organizational Culture and Leadership. San Francisco, Jossey-Bass.

Schein, E. (1996)

'Culture: the missing concept in organizational studies', *Administration Science Quarterly*, 41, 229–40.

Schein, E. (1992)

Organizational Culture and Leadership (2nd edition). San Francisco, Jossey-Bass.

Sheridan, J. (1992)

'Organisational culture and employee retention', *Academy of Management Journal*, 35 (5), 1036–1056.

Swart, J., Kinnie, N. and Purcell, J. (2003)

People and Performance in Knowledge-Intensive Firms. CIPD, London.